MICHAEL DAUGHERTY
MONK IN THE KITCHE

FOR SOLO PIANO
(2001)

HENDON MUSIC

BOOSEY&HAWKES

AN IMAGEM COMPANY

DISTRIBUTED BY

HAL•LEONARD®
CORPORATION
7777 W. BLUEMOUND RD. P.O. BOX 13819 MILWAUKEE, WI 53213

Published by Boosey & Hawkes, Inc.
229 West 28th Street, 11th Floor
New York NY 10001

www.boosey.com

© Copyright 2001 by Hendon Music, Inc., a Boosey & Hawkes company
International copyright secured. All rights reserved.

ISMN 979-0-051-24646-5

Photography:
William P. Gottlieb, *Thelonious Monk at Minton's Playhouse*, New York, New York (1947)
Photo Courtesy of Library of Congress. Used by Permission.

First printed 2012 by Hal Leonard Corp., Milwaukee, WI
Music engraving by Patrick Harlin

Commissioned by Emanuele Arciuli

First performed by Emanuele Arciuli, solo piano,
at the Miller Theatre, Columbia University in New York City
on November 20, 2002.

BIOGRAPHY

Michael Daugherty is one of the most commissioned, performed, and recorded composers on the American concert music scene today. His music is rich with cultural allusions and bears the stamp of classic modernism, with colliding tonalities and blocks of sound; at the same time, his melodies can be eloquent and stirring. Daugherty has been hailed by *The Times* (London) as "a master icon maker" with a "maverick imagination, fearless structural sense and meticulous ear." Daugherty first came to international attention when the Baltimore Symphony Orchestra, conducted by David Zinman, performed his *Metropolis Symphony* at Carnegie Hall in 1994. Since that time, Daugherty's music has entered the orchestral, band and chamber music repertory and made him, according to the League of American Orchestras, one of the ten most performed American composers.

In 2011, the Nashville Symphony's Naxos recording of Daugherty's *Metropolis Symphony* and *Deus ex Machina* was honored with three GRAMMY® Awards, including Best Classical Contemporary Composition.

Born in 1954 in Cedar Rapids, Iowa, Daugherty is the son of a dance-band drummer and the oldest of five brothers, all professional musicians. He studied music composition at the University of North Texas (1972-76), the Manhattan School of Music (1976-78), and computer music at Pierre Boulez's IRCAM in Paris (1979-80). Daugherty received his doctorate from Yale University in 1986 where his teachers included Jacob Druckman, Earle Brown, Roger Reynolds, and Bernard Rands. During this time, he also collaborated with jazz arranger Gil Evans in New York, and pursued further studies with composer György Ligeti in Hamburg, Germany (1982-84). After teaching music composition from 1986-90 at the Oberlin Conservatory of Music, Daugherty joined the School of Music at the University of Michigan (Ann Arbor) in 1991, where he is Professor of Composition and a mentor to many of today's most talented young composers.

Daugherty has been Composer-in-Residence with the Louisville Symphony Orchestra (2000), Detroit Symphony Orchestra (1999-2003), Colorado Symphony Orchestra (2001-02), Cabrillo Festival of Contemporary Music (2001-04, 2006-08, 2011), Westshore Symphony Orchestra (2005-06), Eugene Symphony (2006), the Henry Mancini Summer Institute (2006), the Music from Angel Fire Chamber Music Festival (2006), and the Pacific Symphony (2010-11).

Daugherty has received numerous awards, distinctions, and fellowships for his music, including: a Fulbright Fellowship (1977), the Kennedy Center Friedheim Award (1989), the Goddard Lieberson Fellowship from the American Academy of Arts and Letters (1991), fellowships from the National Endowment for the Arts (1992) and the Guggenheim Foundation (1996), and the Stoeger Prize from the Chamber Music Society of Lincoln Center (2000). In 2005, Daugherty received the Lancaster Symphony Orchestra Composer's Award, and in 2007, the Delaware Symphony Orchestra selected Daugherty as the winner of the A.I. DuPont Award. Also in 2007, he received the American Bandmasters Association Ostwald Award for his composition *Raise the Roof* for Timpani and Symphonic Band. Daugherty has been named "Outstanding Classical Composer" at the Detroit Music Awards in 2007, 2009 and 2010. His GRAMMY® award winning recordings can be heard on Albany, Argo, Delos, Equilibrium, Klavier, Naxos and Nonesuch labels.

COMPOSER'S NOTE

Monk in the Kitchen (2001) for solo piano was commissioned and premiered by Emanuele Arciuli at the Miller Theatre, Columbia University, New York City, on November 20, 2002. *Monk in the Kitchen* is my contribution to *Round Midnight Variations,* a collection of variations inspired by jazz composer and pianist Thelonious Monk (1917-1982). Other composers who contributed to the project included, among others, Milton Babbitt, William Bolcom, George Crumb, John Harbison and Frederic Rzewski.

The title of my tribute refers to the story that Monk did much of his composing on an upright piano located in the small kitchen of his modest New York City apartment. I incorporate various musical sounds and gestures associated with Monk's music to create a moveable feast of rapidly descending whole tone scales, dissonant open-voiced chords, percussive motivic fragments, and cooking rhythms.

—Michael Daugherty

Thelonious Monk at Minton's Playhouse, New York, New York (1947)

MONK IN THE KITCHEN
for solo piano

MICHAEL DAUGHERTY
(2001)

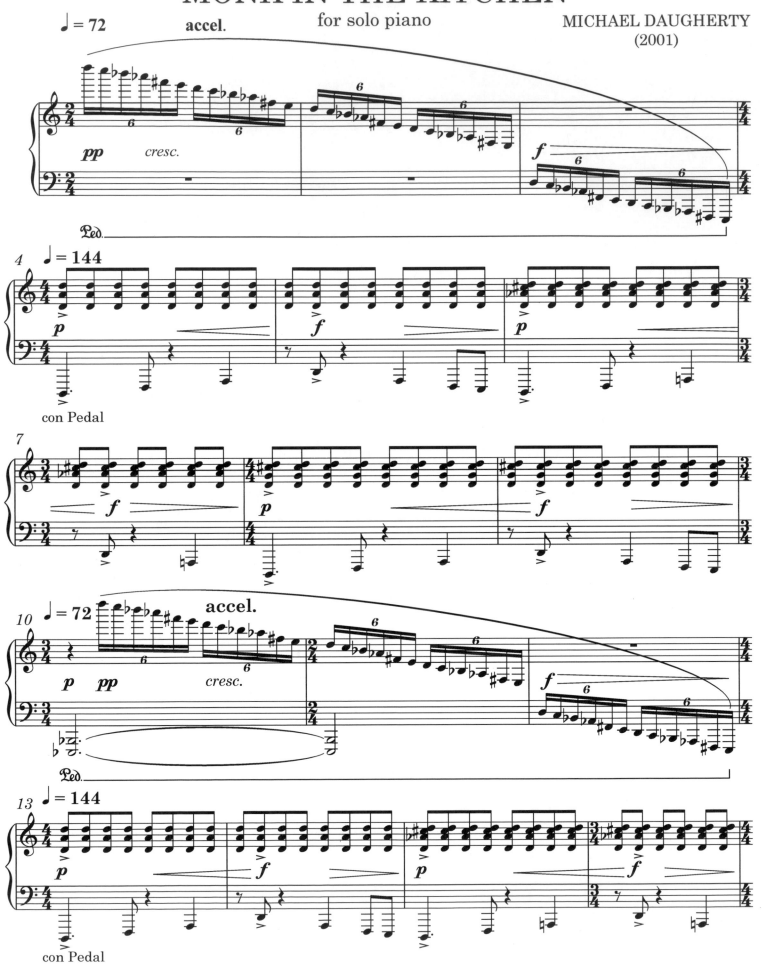

979-0-051-24646-5

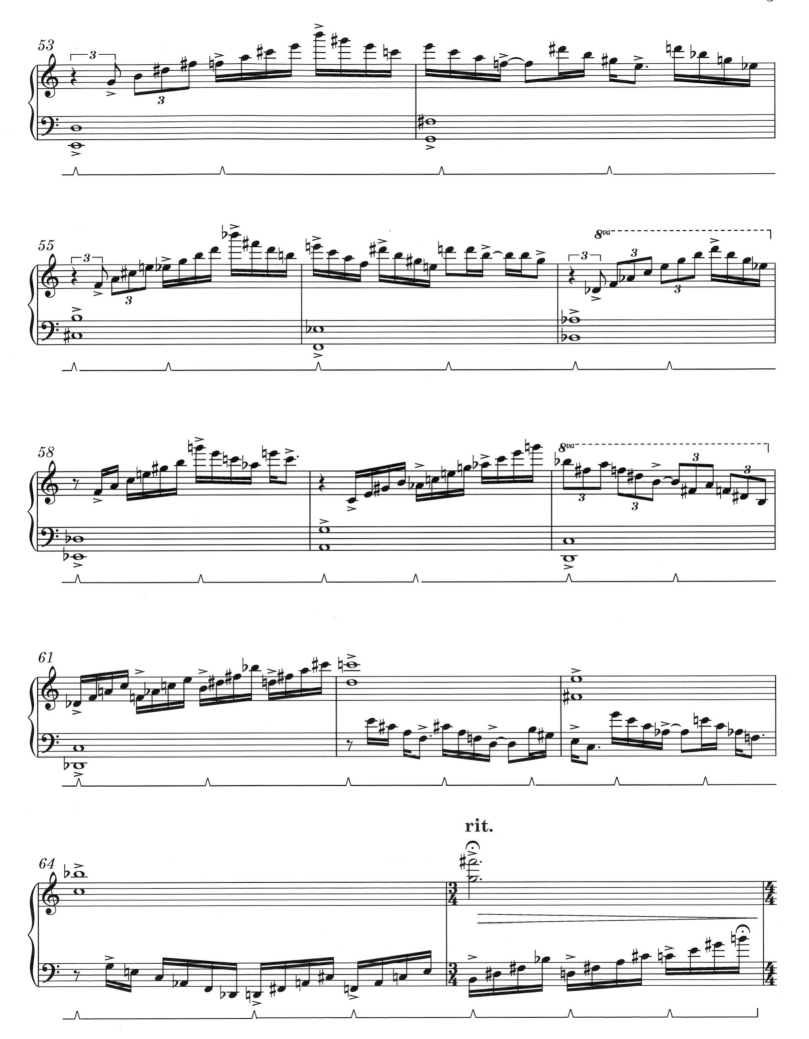

6

* Chords ascend and descend by minor seconds.